For Emily who is still just beginning a life
of discovery and adventure,
and for Mum, Dad and Will for their
continued encouragement and support.

An  A to Z Treasure Hunt

Alice Melvin

Tate Publishing

First published 2007 by order of the Tate Trustees
by Tate Publishing, a division of Tate Enterprises Ltd,
Millbank, London SW1P 4RG
www.tate.org.uk/publishing

British Library Cataloguing in Publication Data
A catalogue record for this book is available from the British
Library

ISBN 978-1-85437-755-5

Distributed in the United States and Canada by Harry N. Abrams,
Inc., New York

Library of Congress Cataloging in Publication Data
Library of Congress Control Number: 2007924374

Printed in Hong Kong by South Seas International Press

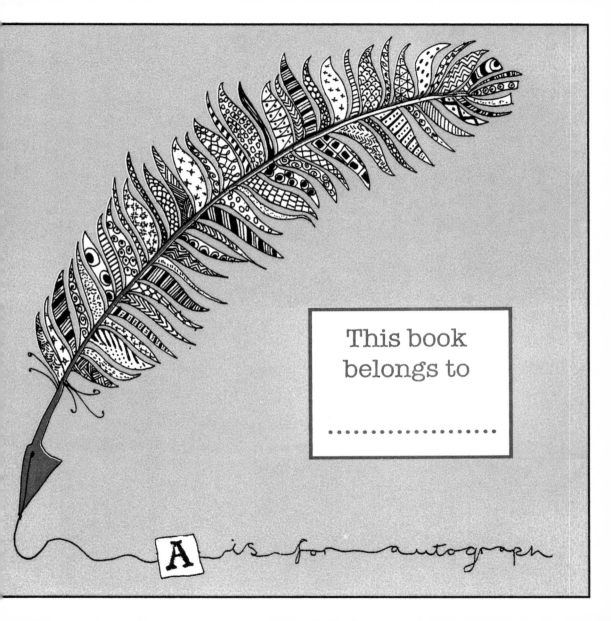

This book
belongs to

. . . .

A is for autograph

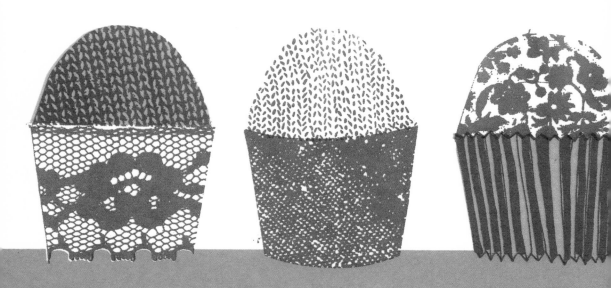

B is for button.

Can you find some buttons to decorate these cakes?

Can you find a coin for the piggy bank?

C is for coin.

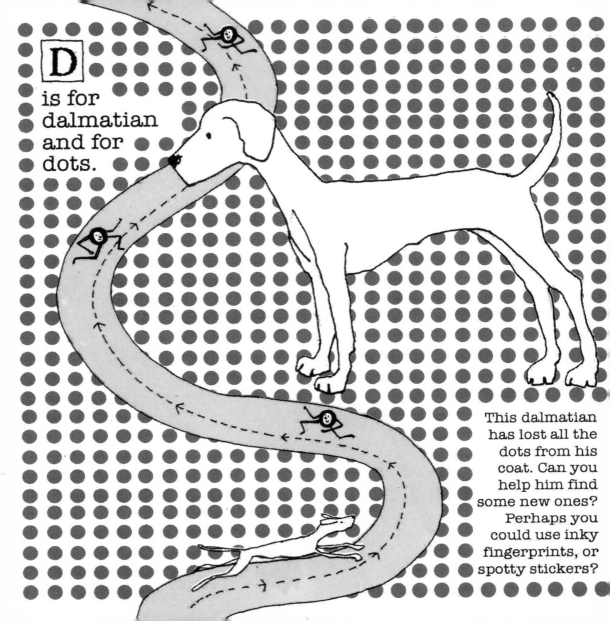

D is for dalmatian and for dots.

This dalmatian has lost all the dots from his coat. Can you help him find some new ones? Perhaps you could use inky fingerprints, or spotty stickers?

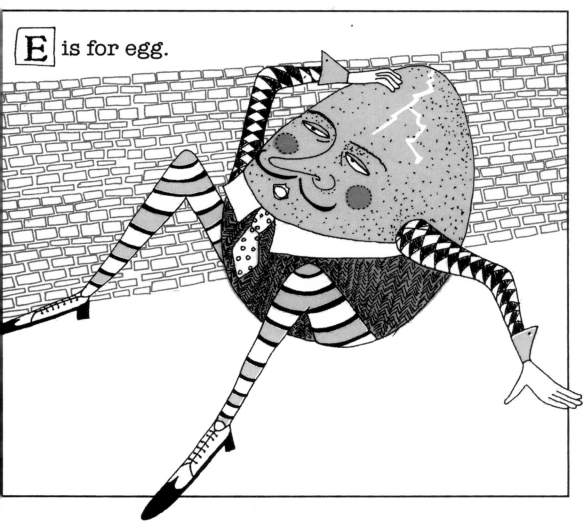

E is for egg.

Can you find an emergency bandage to stick on Humpty Dumpty's sore head?

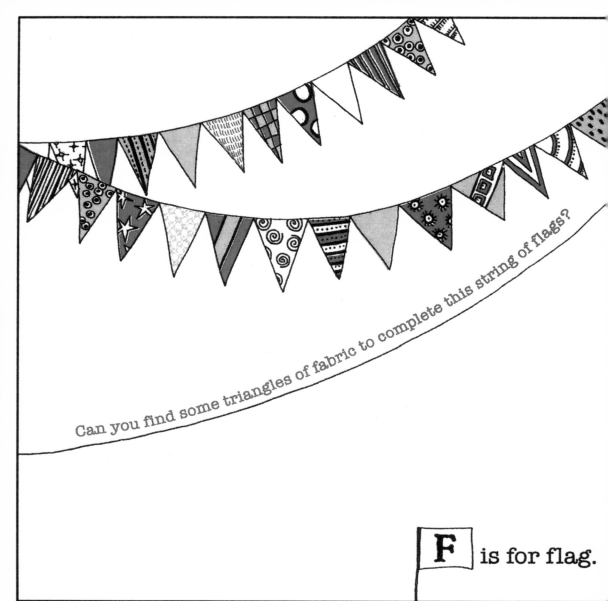

Can you find some triangles of fabric to complete this string of flags?

F is for flag.

G is for goose, glitter, glue and gold!

Can you find some glue and glitter to make this goose's golden egg glimmer?

H is for hand.
This clock is missing its hands. Can you make some new ones?

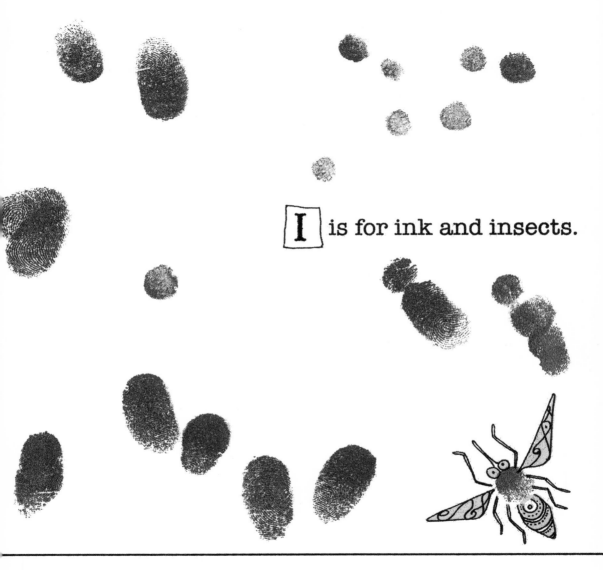

I is for ink and insects.

Can you change these inky prints into insects?

hA ha TEe tee Hee
Ho TEe hOho hEE
TeE Hee HoHo hA HA hAhA
HA tee Hee
bOhO HO Ho
hA hA hee tee hEE Hee
hEE tee hEE
Ho Hee Hee TEe hee
haHa tee Ho haHa

J is for joke.

Can you find a joke
(perhaps from a cracker)
to keep this jolly jester laughing?

K is for king.

L is for

Can you find an autumn leaf to add to this page?

lea

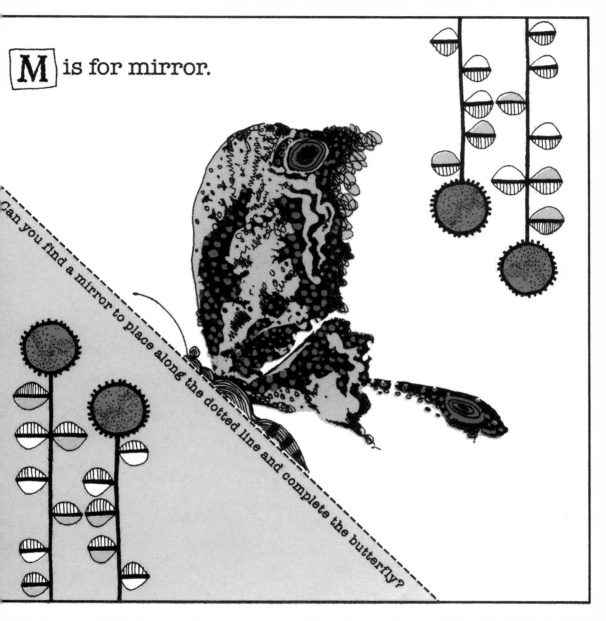

M is for mirror.

Can you find a mirror to place along the dotted line and complete the butterfly?

N is for number.
Can you add numbers from 0 to 9 to the telepho

is for orange.
Can you find some stickers from oranges to add to the fruit in this bowl?

P is for parcel and postage stamp.

To............

Can you find a pos
stamp to add to the la
How about a postal address

Q is for quiz.

1. Which Q is an American coin?

2. Which Q is the name for four musicians playing together?

1...

2...

3...

3. Which Q is a type of bird whose eggs are considered a delicacy?

Can you find the answers to these quiz questions?

R is for ribbon.

Can you find some ribbon to attach to these presents?

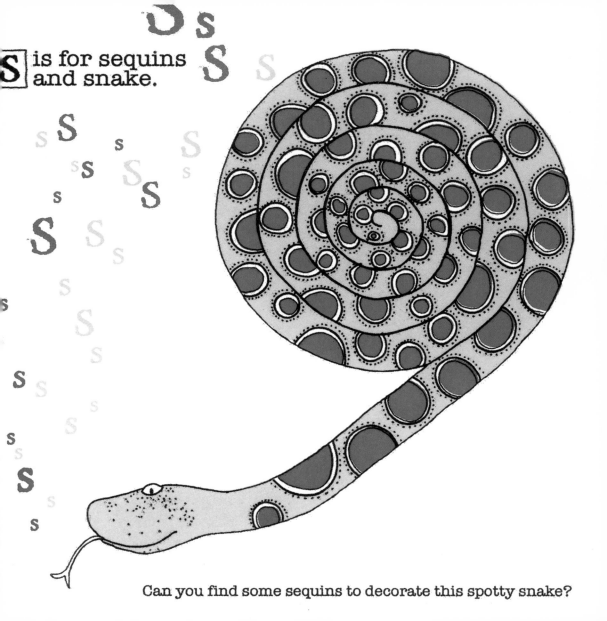

S is for sequins and snake.

Can you find some sequins to decorate this spotty snake?

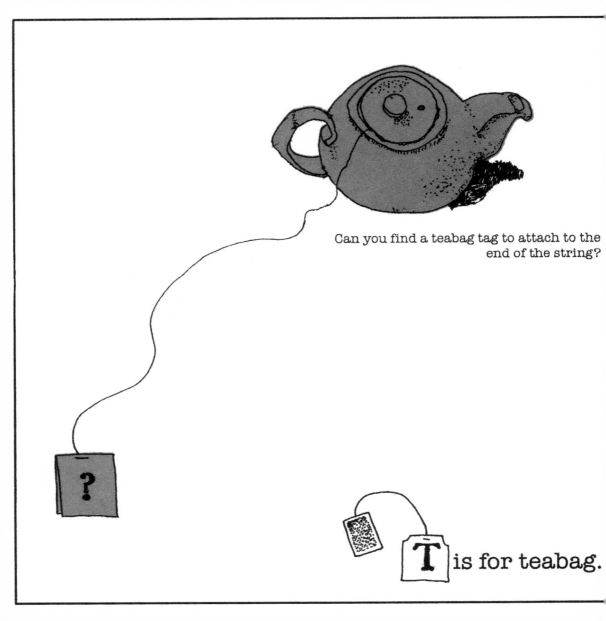

Can you find a teabag tag to attach to the end of the string?

T is for teabag.

V is for view.

Can you find a view that you like? Now draw it in the window.

Can you cut up some wrapping paper to make washing for this line?

 is for washing and wrapping paper.

Y is for you.

YOGHURT

YAM

YULE LOG

YOURSELF

YACHT

YUKKA

YAK

Can you find an image of yourself to add to the gallery? How about drawing a self-portrait?

Congratulations!

You can now find some $\boxed{Z}$s after completing the A to Z Treasure Hunt